Dual Poet Readers: Four

Dual Poet Readers: Four

Rosmarie Waldrop
Damien Lennon

Published by hardPressed poetry, Ireland
http://hardpressedpoetry.blogspot.com/
hardpressedpoetry@gmail.com

Acknowledgments
Rosmarie Waldrop's poems were first printed in
the online or print magazines Alligatorzine,
Bomb, Caketrain, Columbia Poetry Review,
Datableed, Gesture, and 2nd Stutter.

IN ANYONE'S LANGUAGE, AGAIN

Rosmarie Waldrop

1
SILENCE

Your silence which. With a question of punctuation. Seems to repeat. Elsewhere a long complicated life. Syllable by syllable isn't. The slightest pause. What I wanted and. Therefore this curving to tell you.

2
ERROR

What's called a normal. Life a series how long. of grainy errors. Irritating if you feel that way. About errors. Rather than be afraid of words or not really. Afraid but a sense on an empty stomach. Of having already said more. Hauled water from. Than was there. Or that a task could. While it happens to you. Circumscribe. The most terrible things happen.

3
NOUNS

You might grasp at. For safety. A point of view
agreeing. Like a verb, having to, with whatever
you do. But disturbing nothing. Or in rocky
terrain only. When the dark by any other name.
Would washing your hands help you with.
Illusions pale as, but contingent on, the roar. In
the ear. When you talk about winter, your refusal.
To talk in my language. It helps, even if it
distracts, to go with nouns. To have that choice.
Even bold ones like "love."

4
ALREADY DISTANCE

Not being able to decide or measure. The space I had given to you. A weakness that could appeal. Drift could do that. To weakness. Work was to be done. With writing, with the endless sentence. A sandy feel to the skin and along with it. Not matching my all thumbs to your thumb. And motes of dust.

5
PUNCTUATION

Not just a blind pause. As if it had force. Like
prepositions, attentive to. In writing that is. To
everything except meaning. Or dawn. Taking
your hand, or someone else's. Not like a name
that's been spilled. More having an interest in
facts, or Shakespeare. Though always: the rain.

6
COMMAS

What had periods of reflection to do with it, or
commas. Long curving roads. a sense of sequence.
Hoping to come closer, and I don't mean to the
single pore. Was howling up the wrong, headed
south for trouble, hollow tree. Because I don't
want to. Get anywhere. Inward and awkward
become formidable power.

7
INTENTIONS

I can't being heavier now. Attribute. Bad
intentions to you. Because pressed. Silent as when
sleep comes. You're so totally without. Intentions
altogether and unable. To use not drifting either.
Though known as cold or. Flat words could.
Come to mean disarmed.

8
DETOUR

The telephone calls, there are too many. So
difficult too. All these difficulties to work and
work at. Not managing, and you trying to help. In
your way. Your discouraging way. But then, to
float like this, get used to doubt. You have, or
come to, nothing. Not touching, as with a nerve
end. For a liquid to turn to ice when everybody.
Knows the question is not. The feeling one could
have about it. Of strangeness because of how, in
minerals. And not wanting. To detour.

9
THREAD

for Sawako and Eugene

In love, in the wide open, we. Seem to pass
through entire worlds. Though steam rises and
we know we must. By no means, in even brighter.
Light or ever. Let the thread break.

10
POSSESSIVE CASE

It wouldn't be a push. Toward land. As much as
soaring on clipped wingtips. I don't try to reach
by loaded dice, by slow light, glacial. And am not
surprised, in the possessive case, that there's no
land there. Not for me. Though I went at random
and therefore. Could not ever hope to stop.

11
A COUGH

Your name, why go on calling it. Having already.
Struggled, it does no good like giving in. To a
cough. Or trying to. Always in question mode,
leave. An almost labyrinth, the street going on
such a very long time, but even. Even bleary and
inattentive, I feel. The color of air, resistless.

12
TRACES OF SEAFOAM ON THE BEACH

A word in anyone's language. A sound, translated
gesture, an obstacle. Why go on worrying it. A
question, which is not a fabric, Fishing for
whatever's not a word. Could tell of the instant,
you in your chair. The great dreams of the night.
The fog I breathe.

13
THE SKY

I was, had, exhausted. The question. When it is true there is your thin brief voice. And exclamations. But inward where. With an effort of memory, it may look like a garden. But haven't you hurt yourself? By accident? Which, even in an old enough story. As if it could unfold, along the edges. This "V" of Canada geese.

14
LIFE, YOU REPLIED

What shall we do. While thinking about it. For such a long. Ashes of dead stars passed into. Such a very long time that. The book of minerals too. Too hard to read. Driving, not really fast, but. Wanting to. Take our distance. From thinking about it. Which is not

15
YOUR NAME

The question how to open. Your name. Kneedeep
or farther and not telling you, not. In that way. A
map, even scaled down, would help to know.
What I want and what really is. A name. Hugging
the body, not breaking the skin. But almost.
Preferring a lock on limits. Perhaps an amulet.

16
THE NEED

Believing it can be met. To talk in the wind, or to. In spite of cold fingers, this need so exhausting. That more. And more than necessary. One does not use nouns. So I ask myself when even the president. Though the weather turned. The trucks heading north. Taking up the road, the trucks. Heading north, whereas writing. Makes it bearable. Grammar so exciting to put together. Or time. Fumbling with. The need to say "I". Half-heartedly. Pronouns can be so mistaken. So without.

17
YOUR SINGULAR, MY LOVE

Is it what I want? I'd tried not to tell you, not make you see that I'm opaque to myself. Lost among electrons and protons and neutrons, arms tangled with legs. Precipitate fear that writing, though I'm waiting for it, would make me a shadow. Or are we already? And still not worthy of the dark?

ERASED REFERENT

One must think of, but finally, I had to agree, not
walk around naked, not in body or spirit. Not
write about, when what is a word, at the risk of
disconnection no longer ask. What it would take.
Acknowledge the dark, though with dreams in
color and. If still possible. Moist skin against the
page.

EXCESS OF AIR

And so ask: winter? this winter? Not with writing
pressing in. A variety of large and empty, but
perhaps only a tone. Whereas winter means
already distance, break of energy. Regardless of
kisses, snow. Weighing down the branches, not
feeling.

CONJUNCTIONS AND CONSTITUENTS

Love, lord of. Such a silly and out loud. To disperse a crowd for a sentence when a tulip is a tulip. Not only in Holland. Tried to approach. But what of the dishevelment and intermittence? I've been living on the verso of. What shall we, or positive joy? Slow says the body across the dream.

give the void its colours

Damien Lennon

sound into
the knowhere

the nohow
the lore

nothings ring
in each

in nothing music
in nothing speech

before
the silence

what
lies

wall to wall

against
the voiding space

and between walls
murmurs

dig the word
authorize

rig tight tales
comfort all

outside walls
far

look metic
marvel

how alien you are

being has recoiled
back to blurred infinitives
evanescent hints

to Paris for John
in an urn

to Edinburgh
for a reunion

sinew bone and tissue
gone

bleed the word
a palette of liar's blood

good

pigment to
give the void its colours

alphabet of living
limit and mystery

abacus lullaby
linear history

A, B, C,
1, 2, 3,

and so on

dream soup in a can

words came from no
where through

us
conduits

out into the bare
world as if

in the name of the nada
the blank sheet face
the pure white unit

nothing

nada be thy name
the great white pursuit
leviathan absolute

nothing

thy nada come
on the quick tongue
on the loom of lies

nothing: the stem,
the leaves: nothing; nada, no thing

nada to be done

with the starched press
white-yarn-canvass
nada, nothing, bless

then
our premises slip
to their logical deaths

effaced
like yesterday's special
wiped off the slate

shipwrecked we lie
and pray to the ghost
in the stairs of our hearts

come nothing
come out of nothing

our nullpunkt

a bare where
a bare here

what
ever

know only this
the sky is whyless
the wind is simple

the space
I am
in

where
does it
stop

here
else

where
is

nothing
pure

bar
that

nothing
itself

grip words like
a pizza box in high winds

cleanly break dactyls in
the sink of the mind

struggle
only

there is no mute trust
silence does not believe in us

set
against the

black
eternal
hole

sole thing that
makes

empty
nothing
something

the angel of history
and its tomb

oracular leaves
strewn over catacombs

try to leave then

fragment and ruin
the angel cannot turn

ab-ground
    zero

where
    no

is
    ever

no ones

and
their minds

and
their tongues

telling themselves
from themselves

past all cogitation
all sensation
all toil

peace

the wind is home
not a sound is
those eyes

the fullness of
all things

the emptiness
of all things

the mind figures
the names of leaves

of lies

are they
our names

are they
no names

moon ocean grass and sand
sudden light in the roof of the mind
still antecedent persistent peace

whose eyes protest
all emptiness

i

no ideal vernacular
no *ur*-tongue

no things
let alone ideas

best stack
columns of

broken vocables
and

hope or not
they don't collapse

zZzzz ...
zero
NO

w ...
she
where
here
her
or
nope
he
or
her
o

o

     living
     electric
     sound
     of
     noteverything
     y va
ever
     amen

look up above
the angled

    eaves

the azure deep
inverse

    erasure
    of

    moon

gulls glide
like

    spoons over
    clean tables

y nada
  y pues

it always
  is

turn the words
over and over

return them
under the

hammer of
a question mark

they crack under the pressure
they will never assure

at the steeple's crux
above hard flux and complex
nothing blows so cold

in the Salle
Coupole

incinerated
memories

enormous void
and paralysis

man in state
burns

the void swells
the cupula

courage

trace the map
of silence

I
  sky
  stars
  stare

eye
  ever
  y
  where

the hero of
the broken fall
knows

no one
falls on

too much

too
                much

even this

live

en-dehors-en-dedans

the instant
in absolute

the absolute
in instant

look
no further

the
ding an sich

is

the look

almighty moment
dangling from our premises
like rain from a chute

and now is
no

moon

no sun
is

now
cloudless

blue

       star lidless
       stopless

       spark

       whyless
       sky

       whatlessness of
       all

       detail eye

blue
all

a globe
of space

of topos
of place

because
the look

Rosmarie Waldrop (born August 24, 1935), née Sebald, is a contemporary American poet, translator and publisher. Born in Germany, she has lived in the United States since 1958. She has lived in Providence, Rhode Island since the late 1960s. Waldrop is coeditor and publisher of Burning Deck Press, as well as the author or coauthor (as of 2006) of 17 books of poetry, two novels, and three books of criticism.

Damien Lennon was born in Kilkenny and has lived in Paris and New York before settling in Dublin. He's a writer, experimental spontaneous composer/improviser, and bass player, a teacher of modernist literature, philosophy, and intellectual history, husband and a father of three children. He currently lectures at Dublin Business School. Since 2008 he has also regularly taught/tutored at UCD in both the School of Philosophy and the School of English. In addition, he works in UCD's pilot Philosophy in Schools programme, which cultivates practical philosophical application in primary and secondary schools in Ireland for the first time in the history of the State. He has recorded with improvising musical trio Zeropunkt/¡NO! This is his first book publication.